Girl in the Know

Your Inside-and-Out Guide to Growing Up

WRITTEN BY Anne Katz, R.N., Ph.D.

ILLUSTRATED BY Monika Melnychuk

Contents

Girl on the Grow

You're growing up, and that means lots of firsts — first period, first bra, first kiss, just to name a few. It's an exciting time, but it can be a bit overwhelming, too. Being prepared for these changes, the obvious physical ones and the subtler emotional ones, is really important.

Maybe you've talked to your mom or older sister or cousin about what to expect, or you and your friends have dished, sharing everything and anything you know. There'll be advice coming at you from everywhere, and lots of what you'll hear will be true. But you might also hear some stuff that isn't right. This book will set things straight.

This book talks about the changes in the whole of you, starting with the changes in your body. You'll get the facts on bra fitting and your period, including how to deal with it, when to expect it and even what to do if it shows up unexpectedly.

Then it gets into the hard-to-see stuff, your mind and your feelings. Read about how good friends and family can keep you grounded and give you a boost as you reach for the stars, and pick up a tip or two on navigating the changes in your relationships. And see how exploring new things, pursuing your interests and opening your mind to different ideas help you learn more about yourself and the world around you.

Last, but definitely not least, this book maps out the hows and whys of taking care of yourself, inside and out. Up for taking on more responsibility? Get the scoop on what it means to eat well and be active, be a body hygiene-ius and keep safe.

Ready to grow? Read on for all you need to know about keeping your body and yourself at your be-YOU-tiful best!

YOUR BODY:
The Ins and Outs

Before you can learn how to take care of your body, you need to *know* your body. You probably covered head, shoulders, knees and toes in kindergarten, but as you get older, some parts you might not have thought much about before will become more important. So let's take a look. Hair color, skin color, height, weight, shape and features might be different girl to girl, but the basics — what makes girls *girls* — are the same. You might use different names for these parts of your body, but you should also know their proper names — even if they might sound funny. Here's what you share with every girl on the planet ...

On the outside

Breasts: Each breast has a nipple, the part that sticks out, with an areola around it.

The vulva: It's made up of folds of skin; the labia majora (big lips) and the labia minora (small lips). At the front of the labia minora, there's the clitoris, an organ that on the outside appears to be about the size of a pea. Made up of thousands of nerves, the clitoris is super sensitive to the touch.

The mons: Covering the pubic bone, the mons is essentially fatty padding. It's the area that gets covered in pubic hair.

The vagina: Located at the back of the labia minora, this opening leads to the internal sexual organs. Most of the vagina is actually tucked away inside the body. This is where you insert a tampon when you have your period and also where the penis goes during sex.

The urethra and anus: The urethra is where urine exits the body, and the anus is where bowel movements pass. Although these parts aren't girl-specific (boys have them, too), their location next to the vagina makes girls' hygiene especially important. After going to the bathroom, be sure to wipe from front to back — urethra to anus — to prevent the spread of germs.

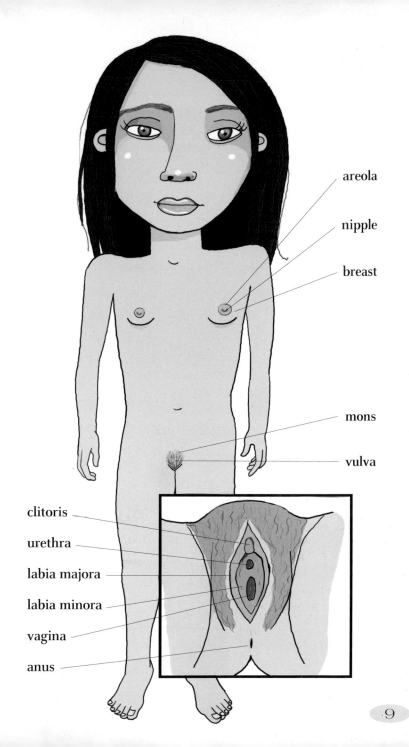

areola

nipple

breast

mons

vulva

clitoris

urethra

labia majora

labia minora

vagina

anus

9

On the inside

The uterus: This amazing, pear-sized organ sits on top of the vagina. Unlike some other organs, like your heart or lungs, you usually can't feel your uterus, except when you have cramps with your period or when you're pregnant. During pregnancy, it expands to make room for a growing baby, or fetus. The uterus is made up of muscle fibers that do all the work during childbirth, contracting to squeeze the baby out.

The cervix: It's through the cervix that menstrual blood flows from the uterus into the vagina, and that sperm enter the uterus, swimming up to meet an egg. When you're pregnant, the cervix opens up during labor to let the baby pass through.

Uterine tubes: Entering the uterus near the top, the two uterine tubes end in fingerlike projections near the ovaries.

Ovaries: These two small organs contain eggs, or ova. Girls are born with all the eggs they'll ever have. At puberty, the ovaries kind of wake up, and every month one or more of those eggs mature. The mature egg is released, falls into the uterine tube and travels to the uterus. If it doesn't meet up with sperm and isn't fertilized, then the egg is washed away with the lining of the uterus as your period. If the egg has been fertilized and you become pregnant, the tiny group of cells, or embryo, attaches to the wall of the uterus where it will grow into a fetus.

A cross-section of reproductive organs

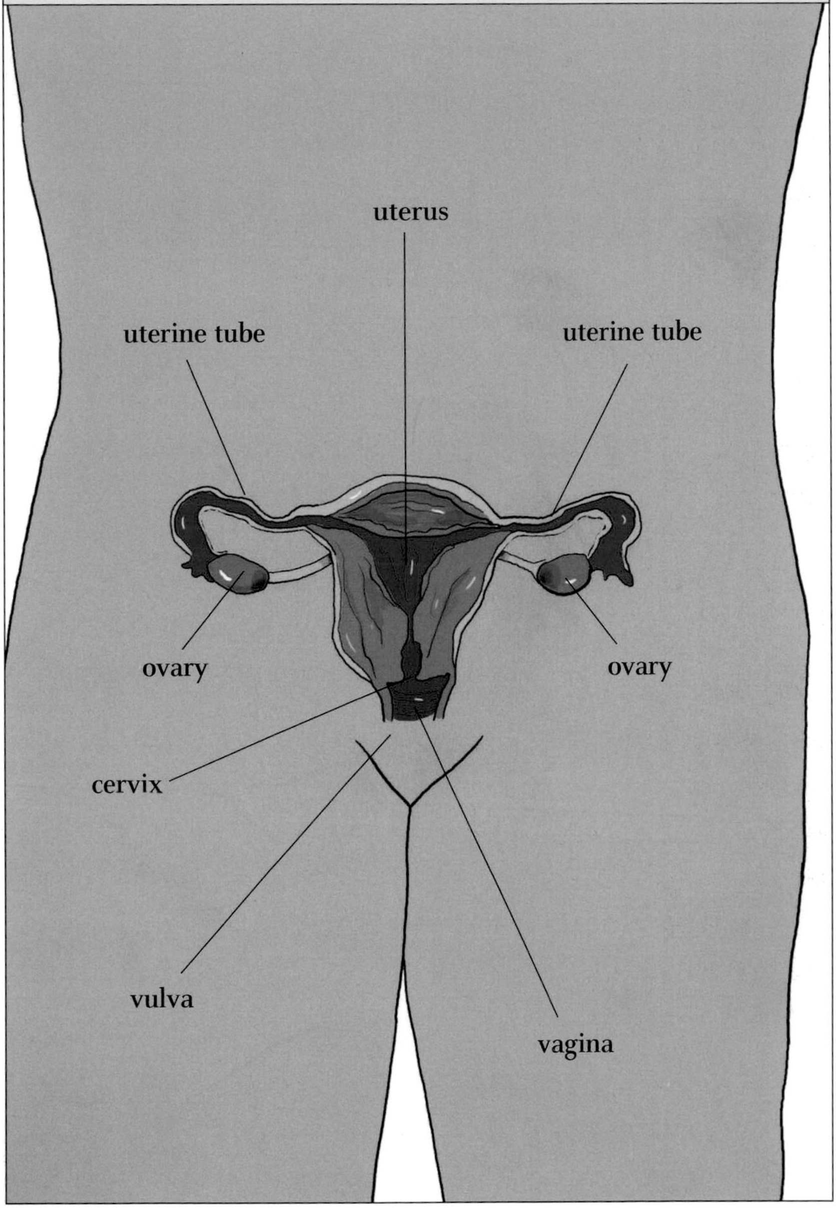

uterus

uterine tube

uterine tube

ovary

ovary

cervix

vulva

vagina

The Skin You're In

Most girls reach puberty between the ages of 10 and 14. Your body is beginning to grow and change into its adult form, which takes time — and some getting used to.

B is for breasts and bras

One day it happens: There's a tingling under your skin, right underneath your nipples (see page 8). They might feel a little sore, almost like bruises. Yup — your breasts are starting to grow, one of the first signs of puberty. There'll likely be some swelling, like cherry-sized bumps, under your nipples, too. This is all thanks to your girl hormones doing their thing. Hormones are chemicals your body makes; they affect your body in different ways, including the development of your breasts.

Your breasts might seem pointy at first, but over the next several months and years (usually till you're 18), they'll get fuller. As they grow, your nipples and areola will darken and might look like bumps on top of your breasts. Sometimes breasts grow at different rates, and one might be bigger than the other, or one nipple might point up or down more. This is perfectly normal and is more noticeable to you than to anyone else — really. Practically no one has symmetrical, or even, breasts. Breasts come in all different shapes and sizes.

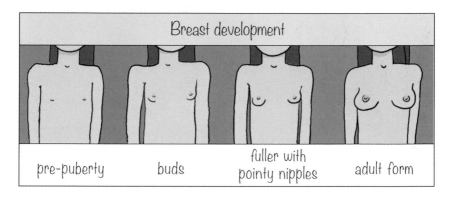

Breast development			
pre-puberty	buds	fuller with pointy nipples	adult form

It's impossible to predict what size your breasts will eventually be, but a lot depends on family history, or heredity — a.k.a. your genes. If your mom has small breasts, you probably will, too. If your mom has large breasts, well, you get the picture. Your weight can also affect their size. Your breasts are made up of mostly fat cells, so you're likely to have smaller breasts if you're skinny and bigger breasts if you're on the curvier side.

At some point your mom might suggest that you get a bra or maybe you'll beat her to it and ask her to take you shopping for one. The kind of bra you choose is really up to you. Some girls start with training bras, which help you to feel comfortable wearing a bra. Other girls prefer to wear a tight undershirt for a while and then move into a sports bra. And others might want something lacy or more grown-up looking. There's a lot of choice out there. Find something you're comfortable wearing and that makes you feel good — as long as it fits you properly, there is no "right" or "wrong" bra.

So how do you know it fits? Sports bra sizing is pretty straightforward; these bras come in small, medium, large or extra large. For other bras, you need to know two things: your band size and your cup size. You can ask the salesperson to measure you, or you can size yourself up at home. Here's how you do it:

To figure out your *band size*, stand straight and wrap a tape measure firmly around your rib cage, under your breasts. Add 12.5 cm (5 in.) to this measurement and then round it up to the next even number.

To figure out your *cup size*, wrap the tape measure firmly around the fullest part of your breasts. Then subtract your band size from this measurement.

- If the measurement you get is the same as your band size, your cup size will be A.

- A difference of up to 2.5 cm (1 in.) means your cup size is B.

- A difference of 2.5 cm (1 in.) to 5 cm (2 in.) means your cup size is C.

- A difference of 5 cm (2 in.) to 7.5 cm (3 in.) means your cup size is D.

Your bra straps should lie flat on your shoulders and be loose enough that they don't make dents in your skin, but tight enough that they don't slide down over your shoulders, either. The back of your bra should lie just under the lower part of your shoulder blades and shouldn't ride up.

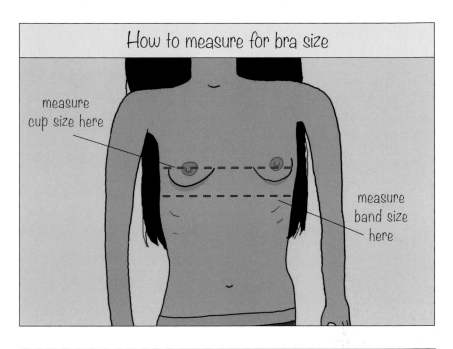

How to measure for bra size

measure
cup size here

measure
band size
here

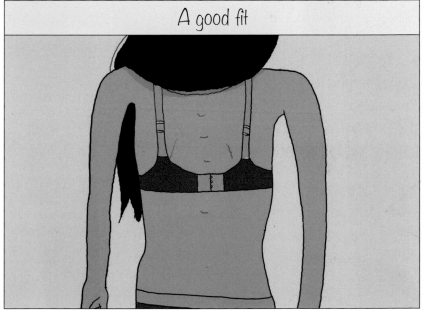

A good fit

Hair there and everywhere

At about the same time as your breasts start to grow, so will body hair. You'll notice it mainly under your arms and in your vulva area, but you might also start to get darker hair on your arms and legs and on your upper lip, too.

In the vulva area, pubic hair starts to grow on the mons (see page 8). At first there'll only be a few straight hairs. Over time the hair will start to get darker and curlier, covering the mons and eventually forming a triangle shape.

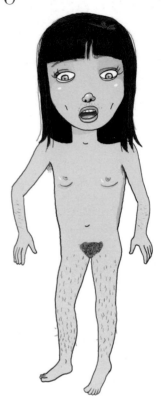

Pubic hair development

Collars and cuffs

Pubic hair is usually the same color as the hair on your head, only darker, so if you're a redhead or a brunette, you'll have pubic hair to match. If you're blond, your pubic hair could be blond or even light brown.

?

✱ Grin and bare it

Many girls and women choose to get rid of some of their body hair, but others just let it grow. How do you decide? Often it depends on what's thought to be acceptable in your peer group or where you live, but really, to remove body hair or not is a personal choice.

There are lots of ways to remove it, but shaving or tweezing is the safest DIY bet for girls just starting out. Shaving your underarms and legs is pretty straightforward. Getting your own razor is a must — no borrowing from Mom, Dad or anyone else. A blunt blade causes nasty nicks and cuts, so be sure to replace it after a few uses. Let your skin soak in the bath or shower for a good few minutes before shaving, and use lots of shaving lotion or soap to prevent razor burn and to keep track of what areas you've already shaved. Tweezing works pretty well, too, if there are only a few hairs to remove — leg hair would take hours! Try tweezing on smaller areas, like plucking stray eyebrow hairs.

Some girls move on to other hair removal methods, including waxing and depilatory creams. Best done by a professional at a beauty salon or spa, waxing can be costly and painful, although it needs to be done less often than shaving, and regrowth often feels softer and is less noticeable. But speaking of regrowth, you need to let your body hair grow back 1 cm ($^1/_4$ in.) or so before you can wax again, which might mean a few furry-feeling days in between. Depilatory creams are chemical hair removers. These can be a bit smelly and messy; most need to be washed off in the shower. There are different strengths available for different areas of your body, like your face or bikini area, so make sure you choose the right one. And follow the directions carefully, especially if you have sensitive skin. Always test it on a small area of skin first. If a rash develops, this isn't the hair removal method for you.

Menstruation, a.k.a. your period

About a year or more after your breasts begin to develop and pubic hair starts to grow, your period is going to show up. There's no sure way of predicting exactly when this'll happen, but there are signs to watch for. In the months leading up to your first period, you might notice that you have more vaginal discharge. It might be clear or milky, and dry to a yellowish color in your underwear. This is how the vagina cleans itself.

A period is the body's way of getting rid of the uterus lining that developed in preparation for pregnancy. When you don't get pregnant, the lining falls away from the walls of the uterus and is shed as menstrual bleeding — your period (see page 10). Many girls' first period is very light; you might notice a small streak of blood on the toilet paper or a smear of brownish discharge on your underwear. This can happen a few periods in a row before heavier bleeding starts. Other girls have bright red bleeding from their very first period; it's different for everyone. Getting your period is a sign that you're healthy and that your body is doing what it's supposed to.

Most periods last from two to seven days, with the bleeding at its heaviest the first couple days. Although it might seem like a lot of blood at the time, you lose only about 30 to 45 mL (2 to 3 tbsp.) in total each month. You can do whatever you would normally do during your period. It's common for your periods to be irregular at first, but eventually you'll get your period every 21 to 35 days. Keep track in your day planner or calendar by making some sort of special mark or note — even a little red dot will do. This way you can see if you've missed a period or if you're close to getting it so you'll have supplies on hand.

✱ Other period business

Some girls also experience other discomforts just before (a.k.a. premenstrual syndrome, or PMS) or during their periods, like cramps, stomach upsets, headaches, sore breasts, bloating or mood swings. Here are a few things you can do to help make your periods more comfortable:

• Exercise. Even just going for a short walk or doing a few relaxation exercises really helps to ease cramps. Feeling a bit blue, too? Not only is exercise good for the body, it's good for the mind and mood: It'll get you smiling (or at least not frowning quite so hard) in no time.

• Lie down with a heating pad or hot water bottle on your tummy. (Or, if Kitty or Fido is small enough — and will sit still long enough! — you can have your furry friend snuggle up instead.) Heat soothes the muscle contractions that cause cramping and helps you to relax.

• Try massaging your belly in a counter-clockwise direction to ease cramping. You can also try gentle massage over your ankles; these are the ovaries' pressure points. And having someone gently massage your neck and shoulders can help with headache tension.

• Some girls take pills to ease severe headaches, breast soreness and cramps. Acetaminophen (Tylenol) may help, but ibuprofen (Motrin and Advil) can be even better. If neither of these medications works for you, ask your doctor what other options are available.

✳ The goods

Your mom might keep the bathroom stocked with a supply of pads or tampons for you, but your period won't always come when you're at home. It's a good idea to carry something with you in your bag and keep a few supplies in your locker at school. If your period catches you off guard and no one you know is around, don't worry. You can do what girls and women have done for ages: Get some toilet paper or paper towel and fold it into a pad shape. It'll do the job till you get home.

The DIY TP pad

1. Tear off a strip of toilet paper as long as your arm.

2. Fold it up, making a narrow rectangle, till you have four squares left.

3. Place the pad in your underwear and wrap the rest of the TP around the gusset.

Mission accomplished!

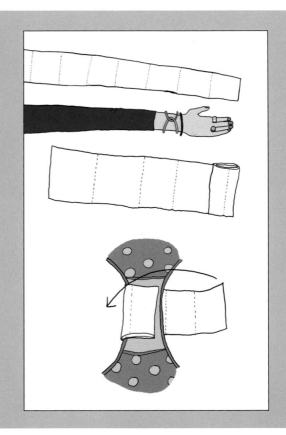

What protection you use when you have the choice will depend on you and the women in your life who give you advice.

• *Pads* come in all shapes, sizes and absorbencies. Most have a sticky strip on the underside to keep them in place in your underwear; some even have protective side flaps, or wings, that wrap around the gusset to keep it clean.

• *Panty liners* are very thin pads that work well if your period is super light or near the end when you just have a little bit of spotting.

• *Tampons* are tight little rolls of absorbent material that are inserted into the vagina (see page 8). Some tampons have cardboard or plastic applicators, while others are inserted using only your fingers. Because they're tucked inside, you won't have to worry about them slipping out of place or leaking. Some girls are able to use tampons from the very first day of their very first period, but others need a bit more practice to get the hang of them. Most times it's just a matter of getting the angle right; placing a clean finger in your vagina will give you an idea of where the tampon needs to go.

• A *menstrual cup* is a rubber gizmo that looks like an upside-down bell. It's inserted into the vagina so that it lies over the cervix to collect the blood (see page 10). To empty the cup, you remove it and pour the menstrual blood out into the toilet, and then wash

the cup before reinserting it. Totally reusable, the menstrual cup is way more environmentally friendly than disposable pads or tampons, but you need to be very comfortable with your girl parts to be able to place it properly.

• *Cloth pads* are another environmentally friendly option. These washable and reusable pads are made from absorbent cotton — probably exactly like the pads your great-grandmother used!

During the day, pads and tampons should be changed every three to four hours, but it's okay to wear a pad all night while you sleep. In the 1980s, there was a big scare when some women got really sick with an infection called toxic shock syndrome (TSS) after wearing super-absorbent tampons made out of a special kind of foam. Those tampons aren't available anymore, but there's still a slight risk of TSS if you leave a tampon in for six or more hours or if you forget to remove a tampon at the end of your period. If you can't get hold of the string to pull the tampon out, don't panic; see your doctor or go to the hospital to have it removed. (It might feel embarrassing, but it actually happens more often than you think, and doctors and nurses have seen it all.)

Supply 411

• Always wash your hands before and after changing a pad, tampon or menstrual cup.

• Always use unscented products. The scented ones can cause irritation.

• Never flush used pads, panty liners or tampon applicators down the toilet. Roll them in TP and put them in the garbage.

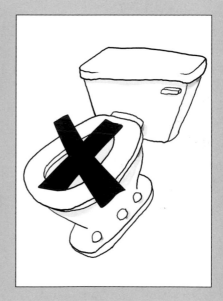

Invasion of the Body Snatchers

Your breasts, pubic hair and period are changes you can see during puberty, but there are also changes going on that you can't see. You do know they're happening, though, and sometimes they're harder to deal with ... (And you thought your period was tricky.)

Mood swings:
The emotional rollercoaster

One minute you're happy, the next you're sad. Things that made you laugh yesterday now just make you mad. Last week you had a great time hanging out with your parents, but today that sounds like torture. Welcome to the sometimes confusing reality of being a teenager!

These emotional changes are partly due to those same hormones that are responsible for breast and body hair growth and your period. You might feel confrontational, vulnerable or easily frustrated in situations you used to sail through. This is normal, but it can affect your relationships with your friends and family. Sometimes it can even feel as if you don't really like yourself! Over time your feelings will settle down and become more predictable, but in the meantime you need to learn how to juggle them all. Just remember that you're in good company: Your friends are going through the same thing. So try to be patient with yourself and one another — there's comfort in numbers. If you're all happy–angry–sad, you can help one another through.

Your brain, version 2.0

Hormones are only partly responsible for the changes in your behavior at puberty. Believe it or not, your brain is behind this, too. Just as your body is taking on its adult form, so is your brain; areas that weren't fully developed before are now under construction, and these changes influence the way you think. Decision-making can be especially tricky. Although you understand that your actions have consequences better than when you were six and gave your sister's dolls haircuts (oopsy!), thinking decisions through can still be difficult.

Trying new things and taking risks are part of being a teenager; they come with the job. But because you might not always think decisions through properly, risk-taking can be hit-and-miss. Teenagers often convince themselves that nothing bad will happen to them; they won't get sick, or get into trouble, or find themselves in dangerous or difficult situations. No one expects you to think like an adult now, but this is where conflict with your parents will happen; they *are* thinking like adults. They'll focus more on all the bad things that could happen if you do something, while you'll be focusing on the good and exciting things. As you get older, you'll be better able to assess risk, to fully understand actions' consequences. You'll start seeing two sides to things; this is called abstract thinking. For now, though, the trick is to find a balance — take some risks (the less risky ones) so that you can learn new things and have new and exciting experiences. Just try not to get carried away.

What to do?

It can be difficult to make decisions about all sorts of things, from what to wear to who your friends should be. Here are a few tips to make it easier:

- Talk about it. Somehow when you actually say the words out loud, it's easier to decide what to do.

- Ask your older sister or cousin or favorite aunt for her opinion. You don't have to do what she says, but she might help you see things differently.

- Make a pros and cons list: Take a piece of paper and draw a line down the center. On one side list all of the pros, or good things, and on other the other side list all the cons, or bad things, that could happen. Seeing both sides of an argument can really help guide your decision, especially if there are way more things on one side of the list than the other.

Keeping safe

When you were a little girl, your parents probably taught you stranger safety and explained the difference between good touch and bad touch. As you become more independent and make more of your own decisions, you'll need to learn to trust your instincts, or intuition. If a situation doesn't feel right, it probably isn't.

• No one, not even family or your crush, has the right to touch your breasts or your vulva or your bum without your permission. It's also not okay for anyone to force you to touch any part of his or her body. This is sexual abuse.

• Unwanted sexual comments or jokes or touching aren't acceptable, either. This is sexual harassment.

• No one has the right to hit you or purposely harm you in any way. Ever. This is physical abuse.

• No one should make you feel bad about yourself by putting you down or humiliating you. This is emotional abuse.

If you are being or have been abused or harassed, get yourself away from the situation or person and tell a trusted adult, even if — especially if — the person who is harming you is a family member. None of this is your fault. People who really care about you are supposed to help you feel safe and good about yourself. It's never okay for them to hurt you.

Crush rush

Up till now you might not have given boys much thought. But as you get older, you might start to notice that your feelings about boys and your relationships with them change. That's your hormones at work again.

You might find that instead of being creatures from outer space or just the kids next door, those same boys have gotten sort of cute. Do you get a weird, fluttery feeling when you see or think about a certain guy? Blush when he talks to you or walks into a room? Think about him all the time and find yourself writing his name on every piece of paper you get your hands on? Crush alert!

You can keep it to yourself, share your secret with your girlfriends, or take a risk and tell your crush about your feelings. Could you deal with your crush not liking you the same way? If not, you might not want to say anything. On the other hand, sometimes it's better to know for sure than always wonder. (That pros and cons list might be helpful here — see page 29.)

Or what if someone has a crush on you but you don't feel the same way? What do you do? Treat the person how you would want to be treated — be honest and kind. Gently explain that you just don't feel the same way.

And what if your crush is a she, not a he? Your teens are for figuring out who you are and whom you're attracted to. All of your relationships — including your friendships with your girlfriends — are more intense, and you tend to feel things more deeply. If you're crushing on a girl now, it could mean you're gay, but not necessarily. Either way, whether you're gay or straight, your sexuality is part of who you are, and you should be comfortable with it. But if you think you might be gay and these feelings are confusing or worrying, you might want to talk to a counselor at school or your parents or another trusted adult — they're there to listen and lend support.

But crushes, like breasts and periods, don't happen for everyone at the same time. If you're not interested in anyone that way, that's perfectly okay. The same goes for kissing and touching. Some of your friends will tell you that they've done some kissing or even touching and fondling. This doesn't mean that you have to be doing the same thing. You need to feel ready to get that close; don't be embarrassed or feel pressured by what others are doing. There's no rush — really! Take your time and share your kisses with someone you care about and who cares about you; they'll be that much sweeter.

On your own

For many girls, part of daydreaming about their crush involves touching themselves, especially their breasts or vulva. This is called masturbation. It might not be talked about very often, but most girls and women do it — it's totally natural to be curious. Figuring out what feels good on your own is a great way to get comfortable with your body and how it works.

YOUR MIND:

The Brains behind the Beauty

So you have this changing body and you're learning to take care of it, but what do you do about how you're feeling? You're starting to figure out who you are, but with all the pressure to act or look a certain way, it can be hard to just be yourself without wondering if that's enough. How does a girl keep a good head on her shoulders?

Your Support Crew

Have you ever heard the saying "Behind every great man is a great woman"? Let's extend that to everyone so no one's left out: Behind every great person are caring people, whether they're family or friends. Life's a long road to travel, so it's great to have company, don't you think?

We are family

Your parents expect you to be moody as a teenager, but they might not know exactly how to handle you. Just yesterday you were their little girl, and today you're someone very different. They're going to have to learn how to interact with you as you change, and although they can remember how they felt when they were your age (really, they can), this doesn't mean that they'll be good at it. This all takes good communication, patience and forgiveness.

Have brothers or sisters? They might have a hard time understanding what you're going through, especially if they're younger. They'll expect you to play with them like you used to, and they might not be all that respectful of your need for privacy. They'll get it one day, but for now, be patient. Ask older siblings or cousins or close friends how they handled things — they might have some tips that'll help you deal.

Let's talk

Communicating with your parents can be tough, especially when you don't seem to be speaking the same language, but the more you do it, the easier it'll get. Here are some tips to get you started:

• Try to plan ahead — schedule a time to talk. Having a discussion about your curfew when you're late for class isn't good timing.
• Manage your mood. Try to put off talking about something if you're angry or hurt or upset. Take a short time out: Go for a walk or listen to some music first.
• Don't just blurt out what you're feeling. In the heat of the moment we often say things we don't mean — and really regret it later. Think about it.
• Use "I" statements. Talk about what YOU are feeling, not what you think the other person is feeling.
• Focus your argument. Don't try to deal with too many things at once.
• Prioritize. Figure out what's important and what you can let go.
• Listen; don't just wait to talk. When you're discussing something important, take turns speaking and let a few seconds go by before you answer each other.

Your other family

When you're a teen, friends are often the most important people in your world, like a second family. They make you feel accepted, special and needed. A friend is someone you can count on to listen to you and cheer you up when you're feeling down, someone who'll tell you when you're being silly or a pain, someone who'll let you be yourself and encourage you to be your best self.

Childhood friends — friends you've known forever — are really special. They know everything about you, and you've shared lots of firsts. When you hit puberty, though, sometimes these forever-friendships go through growing pains. You might find that you have less in common than you used to. Maybe you're into rap and she's into pop, or you go to different schools and have different groups of friends. Change can be scary, but remember: Friends, even best friends, don't have to be exactly alike. Having friends with other interests keeps life interesting — just think of what you can learn from each other.

Friendships aren't always full of sunshine and lollipops, but this is normal. There will be times when you and your friends argue. You'll never see things exactly the same way as someone else. Talk it out. True friends will forgive each other and learn to laugh about their differences.

Heart to heart

Confronting a friend is always tough — no one likes to argue.
Read these tips over, then take a deep breath and go for it.

• Talk to a trusted adult or an older sibling first, or
   write down what you're feeling and ask their advice.
• Wait till you're both calm to talk.
• Go for a walk or do some relaxation exercises first.
• Talk it out in person and in private.
• Think about what you are going to say before you say it.
• Explain how you are feeling — let her speak for herself.
• Listen carefully to what she's saying.
• Are you just too upset? Think about taking
   a little break from each other to get
   some space.

Clique to clique

Have you noticed that you and your friends tend to travel in a pack? Hanging out as a group makes you feel accepted, and that's a great thing. But what about the people outside your group? Different groups aren't all that different from one another — you're all trying to figure out how to get through this stage of life without getting your feelings hurt. So try to treat everyone the way you want to be treated. If you don't want others to say mean things about you or make fun of you, then don't do it to them. Lead by example.

Feeling the squeeze

As fun as a group of friends can be, sometimes there's pressure to behave a certain way. It's easy to get caught up in what other people are doing and to compare yourself to others. And it can be hard to say no, but this doesn't mean that you should just go along with things or change to be like your friends. Often people who pressure others do it to make themselves feel better about their own actions. What's right for

you? Think back to that pros and cons list (see page 29). Ask yourself who will be affected by your decision; the right decision can keep you — and maybe others, too — from getting hurt physically or emotionally. Would you be proud of yourself? How do you think you'll feel about your decision afterward? How will your parents feel — would they be proud of you?

Down with bullies

Peer pressure is bad enough, but bullying is even worse. Do you know someone who's always mean to other kids, either by hurting them physically or threatening or teasing them? Yes? Then you know a bully. If you're being picked on or see that someone else is being bullied, you can't always deal with it yourself. Tell a trusted adult. If the bullying is taking place online, don't reply to nasty e-mails or instant messages. Print out the e-mail so you have some proof of what's going on, and show it to an adult.

Safe surfing

The Internet is an amazing tool — with just a couple clicks you have a whole world at your fingertips. There's a sense of freedom online that you don't have in the real world, and as cool as that is, it comes with added responsibility. Protecting your privacy, and yourself, is super important.

• Share your e-mail address only with people you know well.

• Never include personal information, like your birth date or first name, as part of your account ID or password. Keep your phone number, address and the name of your school to yourself, too.

• Learn how to block e-mails from strangers or people you don't want to talk to.

• Be careful about chat rooms and the information you post about yourself. The people you meet there may not be who they say they are.

• If someone you "meet" acts weird — asks to get together or describe what you look like or where you live, or just makes you uncomfortable — tell your parents or another trusted adult.

• Never agree to an in-person meeting with someone you've met online.

• Save sensitive chats with friends or crushes for face-to-face meetings. With just one mis-click you could e-spill your secrets to your entire school and beyond.

Turning On
and Tuning In

Growing up is like playing connect-the-dots: You learn something new every day, and the more you know the more you connect to the world around you.

Into the great wide open

Your generation will be the leaders of tomorrow (no pressure!), and now is the perfect time to start learning more about the world and your part in it. Get out there and get involved in the causes you believe in or want to know more about. Listen to other people's opinions and ideas. You don't have to believe in the same things — other perspectives can help you to better understand yourself, your family and your place in the world.

Think about volunteering. You could help out at a soup kitchen, a seniors' home or an animal shelter. Or if it's election time, you could lend a hand with a city councilor's campaign. The funny thing about giving your time and energy to others is that you get tons in return. The people you'll meet will all have stories to tell.

You don't have to leave home to make a difference, though — how about getting your family involved in helping the environment? Make simple changes like switching off lights when you leave the room or turning down the heat or air-conditioning when you're all out for the day. Use energy efficient light bulbs and appliances. Reuse and recycle. Or put your heads together and think of other things you can do.

Aim high

Fact of life #138: You have to go to school. So why not make the most of it? School is a stepping stone to the rest of your life, and will equip you with the skills and knowledge you'll use throughout. Doing well will open the door to college or university or a great job later on. For some, doing well means getting an A on every test. For others, it's handing in work on time and getting a C. You don't have to be the best compared to everyone else. You just have to do *your* best.

But school isn't just about tests and grades. It's also about making and keeping friends, learning about yourself and others, and being part of a larger group. School is a time when you can explore who you want to be and who you might become. Every year you'll grow and change. Your teachers and classes will open your mind to new ideas and ways of looking at the world outside of your own experience.

If you want, you could continue the learning journey by going on to university or college. Or you could travel and learn from those experiences. You could also enter the workforce and learn in that way. You could even pursue all of these options! You have so many choices — keep your eyes and ears open and take it all in.

Reading list

Curious about other girls' experiences?
Read on:

- *Anne of Green Gables*
  by L.M. Montgomery
- *Anne Frank: The Diary of
  a Young Girl*
  by Anne Frank
- *Kira-Kira*
  by Cynthia Kadohata
- *Little Women*
  by Louisa May Alcott
- *Losing Forever*
  by Gayle Friesen
- *Love, Stargirl*
  by Jerry Spinelli
- *Parvana's Journey*
  by Deborah Ellis
- *Princess Academy*
  by Shannon Hale
- *The Sisterhood of the
  Traveling Pants*
  by Ann Brashares

But these are just a few suggestions.
Have your own favorites?
Start a book club and swap
with your friends!

Express yourself

When your heart and mind are full
to bursting with a whole jumble of
feelings and thoughts, it can help
to find a way to let it all out. You'll
learn more about yourself and
reduce stress at the same time. Try
writing in your journal or painting
or drawing — experiment with
different styles of poetry or art, or
make up your own. Make a collage
using words and pictures from
magazines to capture your mood,
or bust out the modeling clay and
whip up silly sculptures or a
miniature of the family pet. Snap
digital photos and have fun
altering them on the computer,
or pick up a musical instrument
and play your heart out — hey,
ever given composing a try?
Let those creative
juices flow!

Keeping upbeat

Life can be stressful, and sometimes disappointment can get you down, but a positive attitude can be a big help in keeping the blues at bay and your goals in sight.

- Believe in yourself and in the good of others.
- Admit your mistakes and forgive yourself. Try to do better next time.
- Concentrate on the things you've done well and the good times you've had.
- Spend time with good friends and family.
- Laugh — a lot. (And learn to laugh at yourself, too. No one is perfect, right?)
- Do what you can to help others. You can't beat the warm and fuzzy feeling it brings.

Ready? Set? Relax.

As fantastic as friends and family are, we all need time on our own, whether that's taking the dog for a walk in the park, reading a book or just vegging out and staring at the bedroom ceiling. Up for a few other unwinders? All you really need is a comfortable spot to sit or lie down. And you might want to wear soft, stretchy clothing, like a T-shirt, leggings and socks to keep your feet warm. Here we go:

• Breathe. Sounds silly, but most of us don't breathe properly. We usually take short, shallow breaths and never really draw air deep into our lungs. So sit up straight or stand tall and take a deep breath in through your nose. Feel the air go right into your lungs. Your tummy should move out as you breathe in. Hold the breath for five seconds and then breathe out slowly through your mouth. Do this five times and feel yourself relax.

• Meditate. Concentrating on your breath or a special word, sound or object and focusing only on that can help to shut out the rest of the world, even if it's only for a short time.

• Do yoga. Many poses help reduce stress and make you feel really good — both physically and mentally. They also help you to stretch your muscles and release any tension, or tightness, you've been carrying around. The focus on breathing is also key in helping you relax.

Setting the mood

Candles and fragrant oils are great for creating a calming mood, but you need to be extra careful with them. Ask your parents' permission first and keep these safety tips in mind:

• Place the candle or oil warmer on a hard surface away from open windows and books, magazines, papers, photos or anything else that could catch fire — that goes for curtains, clothing and you, too.

• Never leave a burning candle or oil warmer unattended, not even for a minute. If you need to leave the room, put it out and relight it when you come back.

Precious ZZZs

One more puberty surprise: Your body clock changes. You might want to stay up later and find getting up in the morning hard. But school starts early in the day, which means sleeping in isn't an option. Your body has to learn to get enough sleep to keep you motoring through the day — to tune out so you can tune in. While you're growing, you need at least 8 hours sleep a night; you might even need as much as 10 hours. Try to get the same amount of sleep every night (on weekends, too). Setting up a nighttime routine — taking a warm bath or shower, playing some soft music, reading or writing in your journal for 20 minutes — can help. Do this before going to sleep every night, and your mind will take the hint that it means lights out. Sweet dreams!

TAKING CARE:
Hi, Maintenance!

Your body is a complex machine, and along with seeing to the basics like bathing and brushing your teeth, you also have to remember what keeps it all going — what you eat and drink. A healthy diet keeps your eyes bright and skin glowing, your mood marvelous and your mind and body revved for any activities you're keen on.

Fuelling Up

Food — and the calories it provides — works like a battery for your body. The right battery (nutritious food) will keep the machine (your body) humming along just as it should.

What the body needs

With all the images of "perfectly shaped" girls and women you see every day in print ads and on TV and the Internet, it's hard not to feel pressure to look a certain way or worry about your weight. So put down that magazine, turn off the TV, log off and listen up — girls and women come in all shapes and sizes. Your perfect weight is your healthy weight, period. But how much is *that*? Well, this all depends. Your parents' body shapes definitely have something to do with yours. If people in your family are tall, thin and muscular, then the chances are good that you'll be tall, thin and muscular, too — it's in your genes. And if your parents are short and round, you'll probably lean that way. In your teens your body changes a lot, and what's normal depends not only on your genes, but also on your age and whether you have your period yet, among other things. If you're concerned about your weight, talk to your doctor about making a healthy eating plan that's right for you.

Good eatin'

Healthy eating is about making good choices. The key is to do everything in moderation — no excluding things, but no indulging in too much of any one thing, either. (Well, except for maybe vegetables!)

The average teenage girl should eat about 2200 calories a day. (If you're actively involved in sports, you can add another 600 calories to that.) This will give you the energy you need to get through a typical day of school, after-school activities, homework and hanging out. According to leading health authorities, to get those much-needed mind- and body-building calories, girls your age should eat 5 to 6 servings of fruit and vegetables, 6 to 8 servings of grain products, 3 to 4 servings of milk or other dairy products, 1 to 2 servings of meat or other alternatives, and a maximum of 30 to 45 mL (2 to 3 tbsp.) of unsaturated fat, like vegetable oil or soft, non-hydrogenated margarine every day. Let's break this down, shall we?

2200 calories

✻ Fruits and veggies

One serving equals:

- 125 mL (¹/₂ cup) cut-up fresh fruits

- 125 mL (¹/₂ cup) cooked or chopped vegetables

- 125 mL (¹/₂ cup) fruit juice

- 250 mL (1 cup) salad of leafy greens

But keep in mind that it's always better to eat the whole fruit than to drink the juice; fresh fruit has fiber and also more vitamins, while many fruit juices include added sugar and preservatives. Try to eat one dark green and one orange vegetable a day.

✳ Grains

One serving equals:

- a slice of bread

- half a bagel or pita

- a tortilla

- 125 mL (¹/₂ cup) pasta

- 125 mL (¹/₂ cup) rice

As for cereal, volume depends on its shape and size, so the food label will tell you how much equals 30 g (1 oz.); it's often about 125 mL (¹/₂ cup) but might be less for something like granola, which is heavy.

You want to eat whole grain products rather than processed or white grain. Heads up! Just because something is brown doesn't mean it's whole grain — it might be made with white flour colored with molasses. Read the food label and ingredients list: It should say "whole" or "whole grain" followed by the grain's name, and this should be the first or second ingredient on the list. Aim to eat half your daily grain products from the whole grain family, which includes brown rice, whole oats or oatmeal, whole grain wheat, wild rice, whole rye, quinoa and spelt, among others.

✱ Milk and dairy products

One serving equals:

• 175 mL (³/₄ cup) yogurt

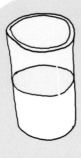

• 250 mL (1 cup) milk
  or soy beverage

• 45 g (1¹/₂ oz.) cheese

Milk is a good source of vitamin D, which helps keep your bones and teeth strong. Drink 500 mL (2 cups) every day, or if you don't like milk or are lactose intolerant, drink a fortified (with vitamin D added) soy beverage instead. Dairy products on the whole are excellent sources of calcium, which is also super important for bone health, especially during your teens. These foods can be fatty though, so try to drink lower fat (skim, 1% or 2%) milk rather than whole milk, and eat yogurt that contains less than 2% milk fat (read the label!) and low-fat cheese that contains no more than 20% milk fat. Ice cream and sour cream contain high levels of saturated fats, but that doesn't mean you shouldn't ever eat them; just don't do it every day. Remember that moderation is the key.

Not just another label

Go on, give those food labels a read — they're packed with useful information!

1 First, look at the amount of the food listed — often it's per part of a cup or by the number of grams. This is the serving portion size. Compare this to your usual portion size. (Surprised at how small their portion size is compared to what you're eating?)

2 Next, check out the calories per serving. If you're eating three or four times the serving size, you need to multiply the calories and everything else by that same number.

3 The food label also tells you what percentage of your daily nutritional requirements is in the serving. Remember to multiply that by your number of servings, too.

4 The amount of fat will be given as a total and then divided by saturated and unsaturated fats. Try to eat foods low in saturated fats and containing zero trans fats.

5 Carbohydrates are also listed as sugars and fiber; go for foods that are high in fiber. These help you feel full and keep your digestive system moving.

6 Give the ingredients a read, too. They're listed according to how much the product contains. So if sugar is first on the list, it means there's more sugar than anything else.

POPULAR NAME-BRAND GRANOLA

Nutrition facts

Serving size: 45 g ($^2/_3$ c.)

Amount per serving	Cereal	With 125 ml ($^1/_2$ c.) 1% milk
Calories	220	280
		% Daily Value*
Fat 9 g	14%	16%
Saturated 7 g	35%	41%
+ Trans 0 g		
Cholesterol 0 mg	0%	2%
Sodium 35 mg	1%	5%
Carbohydrate 31 g	10%	12%
Fiber 3 g	12%	12%
Sugars 12 g		
Protein 4 g	8%	18%
Vitamin A	0%	5%
Vitamin C	0%	1%
Calcium	2%	17%
Iron	6%	0%
Vitamin D	0%	13%

Ingredients: Rolled oats, rolled whole wheat, brown sugar, coconut oil, modified milk ingredients, dried unsweetened coconut, almonds, honey, natural flavor.

*Daily value calculated based on a 2000-calories-a-day diet

63

* Meat and alternatives

One serving equals:

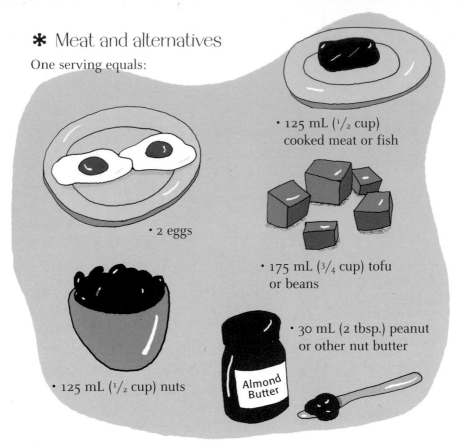

- 125 mL (¹/₂ cup) cooked meat or fish

- 2 eggs

- 175 mL (³/₄ cup) tofu or beans

- 30 mL (2 tbsp.) peanut or other nut butter

- 125 mL (¹/₂ cup) nuts

Almond Butter

Meat isn't unhealthy — it contains proteins, vitamins and iron we need. But it does have higher levels of fat, and often the way we cook it — fried or served with gravy — makes it a less healthy choice. Try to eat lean beef and pork, and skinless chicken, turkey or other poultry. Eat fish at least twice a week, grilling, steaming or baking rather than frying it. If you can, try to eat fresh fish rather than canned. Some kinds of canned fish can be high in salt, which isn't good for you. And mix it up: Eat tofu, beans and other legumes, such as lentils, peas and nuts, instead of meat a few times a week.

✱ Unsaturated fats

A maximum of 30 to 45 mL (2 to 3 tbsp.) meets your body's daily needs. Fat gets a bad rap, but you do need it to help your body absorb vitamins. Fat is naturally present in much of what we eat (think meat, fish, cheese, nuts), so avoid adding lots of extra fats in the form of saturated fats, like butter, hard margarine, salad dressings or mayonnaise. Imagine a plate half filled with vegetables, a quarter filled with meat or alternatives and a quarter filled with grain products; these foods contain enough fats to keep you going, so you don't have to add extra. Other forms of oil like coconut, palm or palm kernel oil are unhealthy in any amount. (Look out for these in the ingredients list of many processed foods, like cookies and potato chips.) Use vegetable oils like olive, canola and soybean oil instead.

✳ A day's eats and treats

Wondering how all of these serving options might work together?
Here's what a balanced, no-cooking-necessary menu might look like:

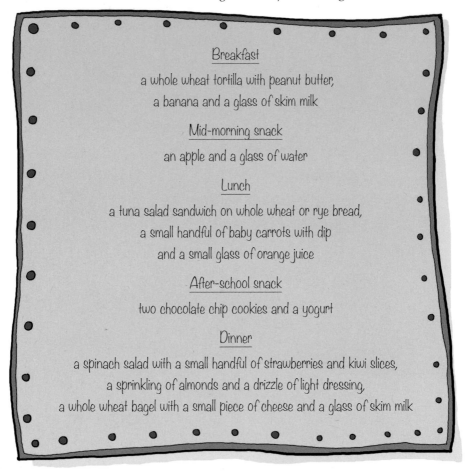

Breakfast
a whole wheat tortilla with peanut butter,
a banana and a glass of skim milk

Mid-morning snack
an apple and a glass of water

Lunch
a tuna salad sandwich on whole wheat or rye bread,
a small handful of baby carrots with dip
and a small glass of orange juice

After-school snack
two chocolate chip cookies and a yogurt

Dinner
a spinach salad with a small handful of strawberries and kiwi slices,
a sprinkling of almonds and a drizzle of light dressing,
a whole wheat bagel with a small piece of cheese and a glass of skim milk

This gives you 7 servings of fruits and vegetables, 5 servings of
grain products, 4 servings of dairy and 3 servings of meat alternatives
as well as a small amount of oils and fats. And it's tasty, too — good to
know if you're left to fend for yourself in the kitchen for a day!

Hands on

As you get older you might be expected to make your own school lunch or lend a hand in the kitchen with meal prep. Helping out can be a great way to learn about and experiment with food. A few rules to keep in mind:

• Always wash your hands with warm water and soap before handling food or eating, and be sure to wash your hands super well after touching raw meat or chicken. Use a nailbrush, too.

• If you're using one, read the recipe carefully a few times, and gather all the ingredients you need before you start.

• Roll up your sleeves so that they don't get in the way.

• Always use the right utensil for the job.

• Use a sharp knife; you're more likely to cut yourself if it's blunt. But be careful!

• Ask for permission to use the stove, and use it only if there's an adult standing by.

• Know where the first aid kit is, just in case.

Munch-a-thon

To see your body through all of the amazing changes that puberty brings, you need to eat and drink throughout the day, pacing yourself so you spread out the calories and keep your body's energy levels even. Listen to your body — what works best for you? Do three meals with snacks in between or six small meals spaced throughout the day do it? Whatever you decide, no skipping meals or snacks. If you do, your energy levels drop, and it's either hello, Miss Crankypants, or good night, Snoozerella. And did we mention breakfast? You've probably heard it a million times, but it's worth repeating. Breakfast really *is* the most important meal of the day, so chow down. Think about it: If you skip breakfast, your body will have been without fuel since dinner the night before. That's about 15 hours! Concentrating at school will be tough, staying awake might be a struggle, and if you're in a bad mood because your brain is starving, you're risking your reputation as Princess Charming. Oh, and your breath won't be so fresh, either. Not quite the image you've been working on? Then get eating, girl!

And don't forget that you need fluids, too. Our bodies are made up of about 80% water, and the water we lose when we sweat or pee needs to be replaced. Aim to drink about eight glasses of fluid a day, or enough that you never feel thirsty. The best fluid is water, but milk or a soy beverage is a very close second. Soda and fruit juice are okay every once in a while, but not often. Soda has lots of sugar or artificial sweeteners (see page 72) and isn't great for your bones or teeth. Some fruit juices aren't much better; they're often made of lots of sugar, too. Energy drinks should also be an every-once-in-a-while thing; not only do they have lots of sugar, but there's tons of salt, too. And they're expensive. (Only high-performance athletes need these, really.)

Meat — not so neat?

Some people don't like the idea of eating meat. Some don't eat animal products like dairy or eggs, either. This can be because of religious beliefs, ideas about not harming other living things or health reasons.

There are a number of different meat-free diets:

- Lacto-ovo vegetarians eat dairy and eggs but no meat or fish.

- Lacto vegetarians eat dairy products but no meat, fish or eggs.

- Ovo vegetarians eat eggs but no meat or dairy.

- Vegans eat no animal products at all.

- Raw foodists eat only raw fruit (they're called fruitarians) and/or vegetables, nuts and seeds.

If you're thinking about cutting out meat, you'll need to find a way to balance your diet and make up the missing nutrients — in this case, it'll be protein. If you keep eating eggs and dairy, you'll still get some of your protein that way, but you'll also need to eat more legumes, seeds and nuts. It might be helpful to see a dietician who can help you plan your meals so that they — and you — are as healthy as possible. Talk to your parents, too; you'll need their help to do this properly. Offer to go grocery shopping with them and make your food choices with their help. And lend a hand in the kitchen; you should take responsibility for your decision — and who knows, maybe you'll teach your parents a thing or two!

A little boost

If you eat a balanced diet with lots of fresh fruits and vegetables, lean meats and fish, low-fat milk or yogurt and whole grain products, you won't need to take vitamins on the side. But if your regular diet is low in any of the basic food groups, you might want to talk to your parents or doctor about taking vitamin supplements. Here's a list of key vitamins, what they do for you and the best foods you can eat to get your fill.

Vitamin	What it does	Found in
A	Keeps your skin clear and your eyes healthy	Dark green veggies, and orange fruits and veggies
B	Keeps red blood cells healthy and gives you energy	Meat, fish and poultry, green leafy veggies, whole wheat grains and legumes
C	Strengthens your teeth, gums and bones and helps fight infection	Red and orange fruits and veggies, and spinach and cabbage
D	Strengthens your teeth and bones	Milk, eggs, salmon and liver
E	Protects your skin, eyes, liver and lungs	Green leafy veggies, nuts, avocados and corn oil
K	Helps blood to clot	Green leafy veggies and cheese

Every-now-and-thens

Some foods and drinks — or more like what's in them — fall into the every-now-and-then category rather than everyday eating and drinking.

• *Caffeine:* A naturally produced drug, it's also made artificially and often added to certain foods and drinks, like chocolate bars and sodas. Caffeine is defined as a drug because it stimulates, or revs up, the body's central nervous system. While it can make you feel more alert and energetic, too much caffeine can also cause headaches, nervousness, difficulty concentrating and sleeping, as well as a fast heart rate.

• *Artificial sweeteners:* These are sugar alternatives. Some health agencies suggest that artificial sweeteners like saccharin (Sweet'N Low), aspartame (Equal) and sucralose (Splenda) are safe, but others disagree. Another product, stevia, comes from a plant. Some people think that this is more natural than the other artificial sweeteners, but studies have not yet shown that stevia is safe. So is it really better to avoid sugary drinks and sodas and switch to something that's artificially sweetened? Maybe not: Drinking artificially sweetened sodas seems to kick start sweet cravings more than sugar-sweetened ones. You might want to reach for a glass of water or milk instead.

Dig in!

Most of us have our likes and dislikes when it comes to food, but a good rule is to try even just one mouthful of something new when it's offered — you never know when you'll taste your new favorite! Take a look at what other kids bring for lunch and snacks at school — maybe they'll share some of their tasty morsels, and you might learn a thing or two about the cuisine of cultures different than yours.

Eat, drink and be merry

Eating is a very social thing all over the world, and in most cultures, big celebrations and holidays — and everyday living, too — often revolve around food. Whether it's home-cooked dishes or restaurant fare, lots of choice is great — you can try different things, making healthy picks where you can, or stick to your favorites and have fun sharing with family and friends. It's good to follow the guidelines for healthy eating, but it's important to let loose now and then and indulge in sweeter or richer things, too. Food isn't just fuel — it's an experience that's meant to be savored and enjoyed, so bon appétit!

Dying to be thin

Remember those models in fashion magazines and the actresses and singers on TV? You know they aren't good role models; they represent a very narrow view of how girls and women should look, and many of them are unhealthy.

Trying to be thin can be a life-altering activity. Your every thought and action is focused on eating or not eating. You ignore the normal feelings of hunger and thirst to control what goes into your mouth and body. Eventually you'll get sick, and it's not just your body that'll be weak and tired. Your mind can get sick, too, and what you see when you look in the mirror is often not what you really look like. You see a fat girl, but what the mirror really shows and everyone else sees is someone who is dangerously ill.

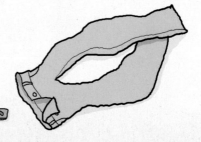

✱ Anorexia nervosa

Anorexics are convinced that they're overweight whether they actually are or not and starve themselves to lose weight. They limit the amount and type of food they eat and sometimes exercise a lot to burn any calories they've eaten. Over time they get thinner and thinner and might stop getting their periods.

✱ Bulimia

Bulimics are also afraid of being overweight, but instead of starving themselves, they binge, or eat a lot at one time, and then make themselves purge by throwing up or taking large doses of laxatives to get the food out of their system. Other girls starve themselves for days after a binge-eating session or over-exercise to try to work off the calories. None of these ways of losing weight are effective; bulimics are often normal weight or a little overweight.

Anorexia and bulimia are life-threatening disorders. Starving and binge-and-purging are extremely harmful to the body and can permanently damage the heart; girls with severe anorexia or bulimia often die of heart attacks.

✳ Compulsive eating

Compulsive eating, or overeating, is another eating disorder, often linked to being overweight and unhealthy. And if your family eats a lot of high-fat foods and snacks, that's how you learn to eat, too. If you sit around watching a lot of TV instead of being active, you might find yourself gaining weight and feeling uncomfortable. Or you might also eat because you're bored, lonely or stressed out. Eating might make you feel better in the moment, but it can lead to even more problems. Do you find yourself heading to the fridge when you have nothing else to do? Turn around and head out the door — taking a ten-minute walk will help stop that urge to eat. Lonely? Call a friend or play with the dog. Stress at school needs to be fixed, too; talk to your parents or a guidance counselor.

✱ Fad diets

Some girls don't go so far as to develop anorexia or bulimia but instead go on fad diets to lose weight. Most fad diets involve cutting out one or more food groups and are unhealthy and unbalanced.

Getting help

If you think about being thin a lot and binge-and-purge, avoid eating or over-exercise, you need help. Talk to a trusted adult. If a friend is having problems with food, talk to her about getting help; if she won't, tell someone. Don't be scared that she'll be mad at you — you could be saving your friend's life.

Keeping it real

Eating healthily starts with listening to your body: If you're hungry, feed it; if you aren't hungry, don't. Your appetite will have its ups and downs, and sometimes you might eat a lot more than you usually do. This might be because your body's doing a lot of growing and you're especially hungry. Other times you might find that you're eating less than you usually do; you could be coming down with a cold or just feeling a bit blue. This is perfectly normal. Everyone goes through this, even adults. So long as you're eating a well-balanced diet of different foods, limiting fast and processed food, getting exercise every day and sleeping as much as you need to, you'll feel and be healthy and your weight will settle at a number that's just right for you. Don't compare yourself to friends or celebrities or models or anyone else. You're you, and it's more important to be healthy than to look a certain way.

Be supportive of your friends and don't talk about who's thin or who's not. Celebrate your skills, talents and accomplishments — things that make you *you*. Don't make fat jokes, and if someone cracks a joke like that, challenge them about why they'd want to laugh at others. Write in to your favorite magazines and ask them to include models who look like you and your friends: Girls who show a range of sizes and shapes and are beautiful just as they are.

Girl on the Go

Keeping healthy is a mind–body thing: Eating good food gives you energy and keeps your body working, and exercising your well-fed body helps keep you feeling happy and your mind sharp, and your heart, lungs, muscles and bones healthy and strong. It also helps you to sleep better and cope with everything you have going on in your busy life. It's a win-to-the-power-of-five situation!

Different strokes

Being active can mean lots of things, from walking to school or riding your bike around the neighborhood, to playing in a baseball league or signing up for a run. And mixing things up so that you work in different types of exercise — aerobic, strengthening and flexibility — over the course of a week is ideal.

Aerobic exercise puts the large muscles of your body (see page 83), especially your leg muscles, to work; it uses your body's oxygen stores and makes you sweat. Anything that makes your heart beat faster and speeds your breathing is aerobic. Running, jumping, skipping, dancing and walking briskly are all examples of aerobic exercise.

Strengthening exercises require the use of some force or effort. All the muscles in your body are used, and you're usually pulling or pushing against something. Push-ups are strengthening exercises — you're pushing your body weight off the floor using your arms. This type of exercise helps to build muscles and is great for keeping you in top shape. Some girls work out with dumbbells or on exercise machines

at home or at the gym for strength training; if you want to give it a try, it's a good idea to get some advice about how to do these exercises properly first. Doing chores around the house is also a great way to do some strengthening — think pushing the lawnmower, raking and vacuuming!

Flexibility exercises help keep your joints loose and your muscles long and supple so you can do these other kinds of exercise without hurting yourself. Stretching, yoga and Pilates are fab forms of flexibility training — they're also great for your posture.

Major muscle groups

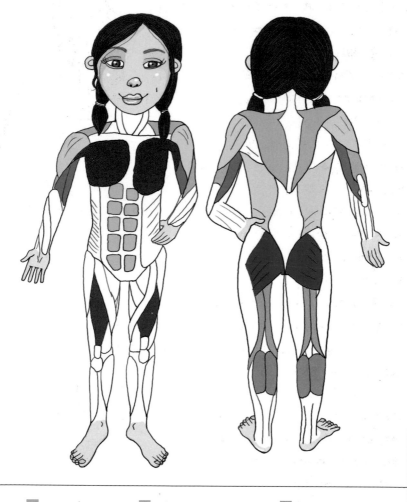

▮ trapezius	▮ triceps	▮ hamstrings
▮ deltoids	▮ latissimus dorsi (lats)	▮ quadraceps
▮ pectorals (pecs)	▮ abdominals (abs)	▮ soleus (calves)
▮ biceps	▮ gluteus maximus (glutes)	

Keeping it fresh

Doing any kind of activity over and over gets boring after a while, and if you're bored, it's easy to find excuses not to do it. Before you know it, you'll be one of those people who sits around watching TV all the time, and what fun is that?! Mix it up and get moving.

Go solo or invite your friends along. Check out your local community center to see what programs they have going on — dancing or martial arts your thing? Or is it swimming or basketball? Rather follow your own schedule? Round up your friends and skate to the park, or play soccer or Frisbee. Or have fun with the family — Mom and Dad'll probably thank you for it.

Do some form of exercise every day for 45 minutes to an hour. You don't have to do it all in one go — walk the dog in the morning for 20 minutes, rock out and dance like a wild thing for 10 minutes in your room after school and rake the leaves in the yard for another 20 to 30 minutes after dinner. Just get in the groove!

Gearing up

As important as it is to get out there and get moving, it's also really important to keep safe and prevent injury — always wear protective gear.

• Wear a helmet when you're riding your bike or rollerblading, and elbow, wrist and knee guards, too, if you're skateboarding.

• Some sports require you to wear a mouth guard to protect your teeth, and others need padding for different parts of your body.

• The right shoes are also important: protect your ankles and toes.

• Wear bright clothing so that you can be seen, and if you're going to be anywhere near traffic, wear reflective gear.

Whatever sport or activity you're keen on trying, make sure you know exactly what you need to keep you safe. Exercise is meant to keep you healthy, not put you in the hospital.

And one, and two, and ...

Always warm up your body before you start any kind of exercise, gently stretching your muscles so they can do what they need to. Stretch both sides of your body. This is part of exercising, so don't rush through it. And no bouncing — this can actually damage the muscles. Long and slow is the rule. Hold each stretch for the count of ten. Take some time to stretch and allow your body and muscles to cool down at the end of your exercise, too. Warming up and cooling down helps to prevent injury and strains, and it'll also prevent stiffness and soreness when you get up the next morning.

Whoa, Nelly!

Listen to your body when you're exercising — it'll tell you when you need to slow down or stop. This doesn't mean you should quit the second you feel out of breath, but if you feel dizzy or sick to your stomach, take a break and see if the feeling goes away. If you can't catch your breath or can't talk, you need to stop, breathe slowly and allow your body to rest. Pain is also something that you should pay attention to — stop. "No pain, no gain" is NOT the way to go.

Make sure that you drink enough water when you exercise. Your body creates a lot of heat when it's working hard and it cools you down by sweating; you need to replace the water you lose. Drink some water before, during and after exercising. Just watch you don't drink so much that it makes you feel sick to your stomach — no gulping! Small sips every couple minutes will keep you feeling comfortable.

SOS

Exercising outside means you're exposed to the weather, and this can mean trouble for your body if you aren't prepared. Be sure to dress properly. If you start to feel sick, stop and get help from an adult. But if it's really hot or really cold, don't exercise outdoors.

R & R

When it comes to exercise, one of the reasons mixing it up is good is that it allows the body to rest and recover. Think about the balance your body needs. Alternate days of hard aerobic exercise, like running, with something a little less intense, like Pilates or a long walk. And look at focusing on one area or major muscle group one day and another the next (see page 83). If you work your legs hard on Tuesday, say by cycling, then focus on your upper body on Wednesday by doing some push-ups or upper body weights. This lets the muscles recover and helps to prevent strain or overuse injury. Had a hard total-body workout, like a game of touch football? Some good stretching the next day will help get out the kinks.

Squeaky Clean

Up till now your parents have taken care of most of your needs. But as you grow older, you're going to want to be more independent and take care of yourself. Read on for tips on how you can be a hygiene-ius from head to toe.

Taming your tresses

If you've noticed that your skin has become oilier (see page 92), your hair probably has, too. Try washing your hair every second day. If it still looks greasy, or if you play sports and are sweating a lot, you might want to wash your hair every day with a gentle shampoo. Use conditioner, but if your hair's oily, massage the conditioner into the ends only, not your scalp. Getting your hair trimmed regularly is another good way to help keep it healthy and looking fresh.

Noticed white flakes? It could be dandruff, or these flakes might be product overload. If it's dandruff, look for special shampoos to treat your dry scalp. If you're using hair products, use a clarifying shampoo once a week to get rid of any buildup.
Hair dryers, curling irons and straighteners are hard on your hair, too, leaving it brittle or frizzy. Let your hair air-dry when you can, and ease up on the curling or straightening — every now and then is fine, but every day's a bit much. Coloring or dyeing your hair can also be rough, but if your heart is set on going Technicolor, get some advice  first — there are so many products on the market that it can be hard to choose the right one. Some girls try home products, like Kool-Aid powder, but the results might be not quite what you expect, so think about it seriously. Still, the great thing about hair is that it's just hair — it'll grow back, and you can usually repair any temporary damage.

Shiny (un)happy people

When you hit puberty, your skin starts to produce an oily substance called sebum. When this sebum gets trapped in the small holes in your skin, or pores, inflammation can set in and — presto! — you have a red bump that gets bigger and bigger until (ew!) a pocket of pus develops. Tempted to squeeze it till it pops? Not a good idea. Popping a pimple can cause more inflammation, making the redness spread, and it can also cause permanent scarring.

Even if you don't get pimples (lucky!), you might notice that your pores are filled with small white or black dots — these are whiteheads and blackheads. The difference between the two is that a blackhead is just sebum that has been exposed to the air while the sebum in a whitehead has not. Again, *no squeezing.*

Keeping your hands away from your face is really difficult, but it's really important. Give in to the urge, and the next thing you know your face is a real mess.

The best way to treat your skin is to wash with a gentle, non-soap cleanser every morning and every night. Use lukewarm water and pat dry with a clean towel. (To prevent germs spreading, don't share towels with family members or anyone else.) Don't overdo it, though. Washing your face more often can actually make the problem worse; your skin will produce more oil if it senses that all the oils are being washed away. Have really bad pimples? Try treating them with an over-the-counter medication that contains benzoyl peroxide. These creams can be drying, so be careful to put them on the pimples only. If this doesn't work for you, see your doctor. She might suggest a prescription medication or other treatments.

If you put anything on your face — moisturizer, sunscreen, makeup — make sure it's oil-free and non-comedogenic. This will prevent more oil being added to your skin and keep your pores clear. And never go to sleep with makeup on, no matter how tired you are — your skin will thank you!

✳ Sunny side down

One of the best things you can do for your skin is to protect yourself from the sun. While your body does need *some* sun, you should NEVER get a sunburn; this ups your chances of developing wrinkles and getting skin cancer later on. Ten minutes a day in the sun will do it; that's all your body needs to make its own vitamin D to help keep your bones strong.

But there's no such thing as a safe tan, and that includes tanning booth and tanning bed tans. When your skin darkens in response to the sun, it means that it's been damaged. Always wear sunscreen with a sun protection factor, or SPF, of at least 15 when you're outside, especially between 10 AM and 3 PM. An SPF factor of 15 means that you can be in the sun 15 times longer without burning than if you didn't have any sun protection at all. Sitting in the shade on a sunny day offers some sun protection, too, but doesn't protect you completely. The same goes for a cloudy day — sun rays still filter through the clouds. Wear a hat to protect your face and scalp, and slather on more sunscreen every couple hours, especially after swimming or playing sports where you sweat a lot. You should use about 45 mL (3 tbsp.) of sunscreen every time — grease up!

Body art

Piercings and tattoos have been part of body decoration for centuries, and what's considered acceptable changes over the years and differs from culture to culture. Ear piercing is the perfect example: Although it has long been common for baby girls to have their ears pierced in many parts of the world, ear piercing in North America among women of Anglo-Saxon descent has actually only been considered a widely socially acceptable thing in the last 40 years or so. Other body piercings are pretty popular among young people now, too, but people your parents' age (and maybe your parents themselves) might not be so comfortable with them. Tattooing is also really popular, but it isn't everyone's thing either.

The thing about piercings and tattoos is that they can't be completely undone. Unless they're the press-on kind, tattoos are permanent (getting them "removed" doesn't work as neatly as an eraser does), and even though piercings can be taken out, they often leave a scar. What might sound like a good idea at the time can seem really lame five years later.

Want to pierce your ears — or another body part — or get a tattoo? If you're under 18, you'll need your parents' written permission. Never go the DIY route or have a friend do it for you. It can cause bleeding, infection or bad scarring.

All ears

Ears are low-maintenance bits — they need just some simple care. Your ears get washed when you shower, but their insides are self-cleaning. Ear wax stops dirt and other stuff from getting too close to your eardrums; things stick to the wax and then the wax makes its way to the outside of your ear canal, taking everything with it. Resist the urge to help things along, though: NEVER put anything in your ear canals. Even cotton swabs can do real damage, so hands off.

Being super careful when listening to music is another key ear health tip: Keep the volume down! You might not notice it till years later, but loud music damages your hearing. And it isn't just hardcore rockers who go deaf — former U.S. president Bill Clinton's high school band performing, concert going, saxophone playing and other noisy activities ended up winning him a pair of hearing aids at age 51. If the person standing next to you can hear the music from your ear buds or earphones, or if you have to yell to be heard at a party, it's too loud. Listening for too long also increases your hearing-loss risk, so go easy on your MP3 use. Heading off to a concert or a movie or have band practice? Pop in a pair of earplugs to cut down the noise — you'll actually hear everything more clearly!

Last but not least, if you have piercings, wash your hands before you change your earrings. This helps to prevent both nasty ear and piercing infections. Cleaning your earrings every now and then is a good move, too.

Say "cheese"!

Not only do you need healthy teeth to eat, but your teeth and gums tell the world about you in the flash of a smile. Think of it as advertising — you want to make a good impression.

Mouthwash is optional, but brushing at least twice a day and flossing to keep your breath fresh and prevent cavities is a must. Some people brush after eating, too, especially if it's candy or dried fruit. Giving your mouth a quick rinse with water after drinking juice or pop is also a help. And remember to brush your tongue! Use a toothbrush with soft bristles, and replace it every three months or after you've had a cold or cough; germs can live in the bristles. Top up your DIY oral care with a visit to your dentist and hygienist every six to nine months for regular cleanings; if any cavities do appear, you can get them looked after lickety-split. Cavities are caused by plaque, a sticky substance that coats your teeth. Over time the plaque eats into your tooth enamel, the tooth's outer layer. If you don't brush and floss regularly to prevent cavities or quickly treat any that form, you could lose your teeth — not a pretty picture.

If your teeth are crooked or crowded, your dentist might suggest you see an orthodontist about getting braces. Many kids today have braces — in fact it's more common to need them than not. You'll just need to take extra care keeping your teeth clean, and avoid eating sticky things.

Hands up

Our hands let us do a million different things. We use them to eat, to bathe, to add expression to what we're saying and to hold someone else's hand. And we also use them to cover a sneeze or a cough and rub our eyes ... Everything we touch is covered with germs and viruses, so frequent hand washing will help to prevent you from getting colds and flu. It's a simple thing, but it's one of the most important things you can do to keep yourself healthy.

Tiny bubbles

It's not rocket science, but here's a hand washing how-to reminder:

- Use soap and warm or hot water.
- Wash your hands for about a minute, or the time it takes to sing your ABCs.
- Rinse well and dry with a clean towel.

Always wash your hands after going to the bathroom and before you eat. Some soaps can be drying, so you might want to use hand lotion. Lotion can also help soften any hard areas, or calluses, on your hands. Calluses form wherever there's pressure; you might have one or more on your writing hand from the pressure of your pen or pencil, or on your palms from practicing on the bars in gymnastics or handling the rigging in sailing. Rubbing the area with a pumice stone or emery board might help, but it's best to prevent them if you can. If possible, wear protective gloves or other hand coverings. Nail care is important, too. Keep your nails neat and not too long, and try to use a nailbrush when you wash your hands.

✱ Chew on this

Are you a nail biter or thumb sucker? It's hard to quit these habits, but keep trying — you will succeed! Here are some tips:

• Keep your hands busy: Carry a string of beads and play with them when you're watching TV or hanging out instead of putting your fingers in your mouth.

• Carry an emery board or nail file to smooth down any rough edges on your nails to keep you from picking at or biting them.

• Try bad-tasting nail polishes — fingers not so yummy, are they?

• Wear gloves to bed to keep you from sucking in your sleep.

• Reward yourself for not biting or sucking. Track the days on a calendar, and after a week, do something nice for yourself.

• Think about why and when you bite your nails or suck your thumb. Do you do it when you're feeling anxious or upset? Try to find other ways to work through these feelings, like talking with a friend or writing in your journal.

Smelling sweet

If you believe what you see on TV or read in magazines, girls are meant to smell like candy or a bunch of flowers all the time. Really, you don't naturally smell of anything in particular. But as you get older, the sweat glands all over your body — but especially under your arms and in your groin area — get more active. When your body makes sweat to cool itself and this sweat is exposed to the germs that live on your skin and in the air around you, body odors result.

Keeping body odors in check is a matter of prevention and care. First, wash at least once a day with mild soap and water. Pay particular attention to your armpits and vulva, where the sweat glands are most numerous. Rinse and then dry yourself well with a clean towel. You might want to use an underarm deodorant or antiperspirant, too. What's the difference, you ask? A deodorant hides the smell of sweat, while an antiperspirant actually reduces the amount of sweat produced under your arms. You can also find deodorant–antiperspirant combinations. These products all come in various forms — sticks, sprays and gels, scented or unscented. There are some natural alternatives available, too, like a special rock-like crystal. And some girls powder their pits with bicarbonate of soda, or baking soda — but this leaves white marks, so be careful you don't get it on your clothes.

So should your vagina and vulva smell like summer rain? No. Not summer rain, winter storms, daisies or anything other than what nature intended. Depending on the balance of healthy bacteria, and to some extent on what you've eaten, your vagina and vulva can smell sweet, a little salty or yeasty. Vaginal sprays or deodorizers, douches and scented feminine wipes are unnecessary, unhealthy and a huge waste of money. They mess with the balance of natural bacteria and make it more likely for your vulva to get irritated and for you to get an infection. If you take care to wash yourself regularly, you won't need any "freshening up" — daisy-scented or otherwise.

Playing footsy

Our feet carry many of us through the world. They're our natural mode of transportation. Take care of your feet, and they'll take care of you.

The most important thing about keeping your feet healthy and happy is to wear comfortable shoes. They need to fit properly, leaving enough room for your toes to wiggle. Wrong-sized shoes can cause blisters or permanent calluses on your feet, and over time they can even cause deformities. (Have you ever seen a ballet dancer's feet? Pointe shoes might look pretty, but they are *very* painful.) If you try on uncomfortable shoes in the store, don't be fooled into thinking they'll soften or stretch — they won't get more comfortable over time.

Keep your toenails short and clean. Clip them after you've had a bath or shower, when they're softer, and cut straight across to prevent the corners from growing into the skin; ingrown nails are painful and can get infected.

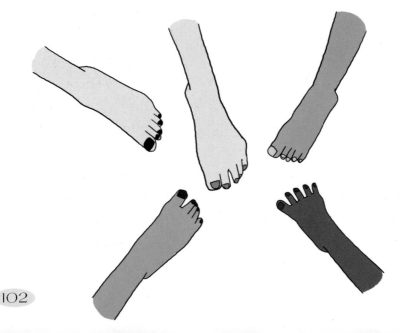

Do your feet get a bit smelly sometimes? Surprise! You have sweat glands on your feet. The good news is that it's easy to prevent odors. Always wear cotton socks when you're wearing shoes; they'll absorb any moisture. And wear shoes made of natural materials like leather or canvas if you can. Unlike plastic or rubber, natural  materials let your feet breathe. (If you want to avoid wearing animal products like leather, stick to canvas shoes instead of other synthetic materials.) Shoes stinky? Sprinkle some baking soda in and leave them overnight; shake the powder out in the morning and — ta-da! — odor be gone.

Baking soda doesn't work magic for everything, though. If you have itching and flaking skin, especially between your toes, you might have caught a foot fungus, a.k.a. athlete's foot. It can lurk in the shower, locker room or bathroom where it's warm and wet most of the time. Athlete's foot is contagious; if someone in your family has it and you use the same shower, you can get it, too. Wear flip-flops in public showers, and spray down the shower stall or bathtub at home with a cleaning spray after every use. Talk to the pharmacist at your local drugstore about the different products to treat athlete's foot.

Checking In

You likely have your day-to-day maintenance routine down pat, but every now and then you'll also want to check in with your family doctor, nurse practitioner and other health care professionals to make sure that everything's on track with your body's growth and development.

What's up, Doc?

You've probably been seeing a doctor or nurse practitioner every year since you were a baby. Most girls keep up these visits in their teens, too. It's good to have a relationship with a health care provider so if you feel sick or have questions, you can talk to someone you know. As you get older, you might still want your mom or dad to be in the room with you when go to your appointment, or you might want to do this by yourself — it's up to you.

Going to the doctor or nurse practitioner can sometimes feel rushed, so if you have questions, it's a good idea to write them down. Start by saying, "I have some questions I'd like to ask. Is this a good time?" and then go through your questions one by one. If you don't understand something, ask again. This is your time with the doctor or nurse, and she should answer all your questions in a way that you understand. If you don't get through your whole list, make another appointment. (This is good preparation and practice for any medical appointment you have.)

Straight shooter

When you were little, you probably had vaccinations to help prevent certain diseases. Now that you're a teenager, you may need a booster shot to keep up that protection. There's also a new vaccine that protects young women against the human papillomavirus (HPV), a virus that can cause cancer of the cervix. Your health care provider may talk to you and your parents about this. If you and your parents decide that you should get this vaccine, it should be given before you become sexually active.

Your doctor or nurse practitioner will ask questions, too — about how you're feeling and whether you've started your period yet. She'll weigh you, measure your height, listen to your lungs and check your ears and eyes. Unless you have problems you've asked your doctor or nurse practitioner about or are having sex, you shouldn't need a pelvic or internal exam. If you do need to have a pelvic exam, you can ask for your mom or friend or a nurse to be in the room to make you feel more comfortable if you like.

Seeing eye to eye

You probably had your eyes checked by an optometrist, or eye doctor, when you first started reading, but it's a good idea to have them checked again when you hit puberty. It's not unusual to find that as you grow, your eyes change, and you might not be seeing as well as you should. In class are the words on the board clear or fuzzy? Do you have to hold your book or magazine really close to see the words clearly, or are the words fuzzy up close but clear if you hold the book farther away? Not being able to see clearly leads to headaches and eye strain. Time to get your eyes checked.

The optometrist will shine a light in your eyes and have you read from a chart on the wall. He might also put drops in your eyes so that he can see into the back of your eyeball. This might sting a tiny bit, and you won't be able to see clearly for a while after, but it's not too bad.

If you do need corrective lenses to see properly, you have a couple of choices. Glasses come in tons of different styles and are a good choice if you only need them some of the time, like when you're reading, or for distance, like at the movies. Glasses can be a great fashion accessory — choose frames that really suit your style and personality!

Need to wear corrective lenses from morning till night, day in day out? Contact lenses might be for you. Contacts are very small, thin discs of special plastic that you slip into your eyes over your irises. They do need special care, though — you have to be really good about cleaning and storing them and washing your hands before putting them in. Even if you decide that you want to wear contacts, you'll still need a pair of glasses for when you don't feel like wearing your contacts, or on long flights or sleepovers, and just to give your eyes a rest. Contacts are also pricey, so your parents will have something to say about it, too.

Gotta wear shades

Your eyes need protection from the sun just like your skin does. Wear sunglasses with ultraviolet light protection — both UVA and UVB — when you're outside, especially if it's snowy. All that white stuff reflects back into your eyes. Same goes for water, so don't hit the beach without them.

More Questions?

Sometimes answers lead to more questions. In fact, that pretty much sums up life — the more you know, the more you want to know! This book has answers to many of the questions you might have, but it doesn't have the gazillions of answers required to cover absolutely every possibility. That's where other resources, or sources of information and all kinds of support, come in.

Turn to people whose advice you can trust, whomever you feel most comfortable talking to — your parents, a school counselor, a close family friend or your doctor. You might even think about including your local librarian on that list. Librarians are a great resource: They can help you suss out the information you need by suggesting books, Web sites or other media sources that cover the topics you're interested in learning more about. Be generous and share that wealth of information — fill your friends in on your newly learned facts and finds so that they're as clued in as you.

Your teens are about being young and kind of grown up at the same time, and learning to be your own person. But even though you're taking on more responsibility and making some of your own decisions, it doesn't mean you have to go it alone. Part of growing up and learning to take care of yourself is knowing when to ask for help. Reach out — the people who care are there for you, no matter what.

Index

To my daughter, Ayli, who sometimes let me guide her through this time in her life. And with thanks to Nicole and Cayly Askin for their honest opinions about the contents of this book — A.K.

For my niece, Madelyn — M.M.

Text © 2010 Anne Katz
Illustrations © 2010 Monika Melnychuk

Kids Can Press acknowledges the financial support of the Government of Ontario, through the Ontario Media Development Corporation's Ontario Book Initiative; the Ontario Arts Council; the Canada Council for the Arts; and the Government of Canada, through the BPIDP, for our publishing activity.

Published in Canada by
Kids Can Press Ltd.
25 Dockside Drive
Toronto, ON M5A 0B5

Published in the U.S. by
Kids Can Press Ltd.
2250 Military Road
Tonawanda, NY 14150

www.kidscanpress.com

Edited by Yvette Ghione
Designed by Karen Powers

This book is smyth sewn casebound.
Manufactured in Buji, Shenzhen, China, in 7/2010 by WKT Company

CM 10 0 9 8 7 6 5 4 3 2

Library and Archives Canada Cataloguing in Publication

Katz, Anne, 1958–
    Girl in the know : your inside-and-out guide to growing up / written by Anne Katz ; illustrated by Monika Melnychuk.

Includes index.
ISBN 978-1-55453-303-9

1. Girls—Health and hygiene—Juvenile literature. 2. Puberty—Juvenile literature.
3. Girls—Life skills guides—Juvenile literature.
I. Melnychuk, Monika II. Title.

RA777.25.K38 2010   j613'.04242   C2009-903896-X

Kids Can Press is a *CORUS*™ Entertainment company